OUR PLANET

Mountains

ZUZA VRBOVA

Troll Associates

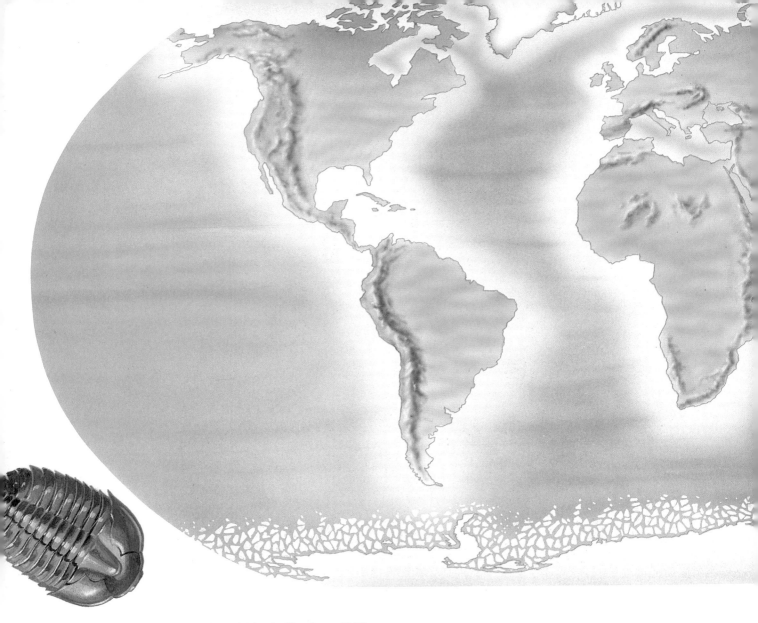

Published by Troll Associates, Mahwah, New Jersey 07430

Design by James Marks, London.

Picture research by Jan Croot.

Illustrators: Martin Camm: pages 12, 13, 14, 15, 18, 21, 24, 25, 26, 27; Mike Roffe: pages 4-5, 6-7, 8-9, 10-11, 16; Paul Sullivan: pages 18-19; Ian Thompson: pages 2-3; David Webb: pages 26, 28, 29.

Printed in the U.S.A.

10 9 8 7 6 5 4 3 2 1

Library of Congress Cataloging-in-Publication Data

Vrbova, Zuza.
    Mountains / by Zuza Vrbova; illustrated by Martin Camm . . . [et al.].
        p.   cm.—(Our planet)
    Summary: Describes the characteristics and formation of the world's mountains and the plant, animal, and human communities that live there.
    ISBN 0-8167-1973-X (lib. bdg.)   ISBN 0-8167-1974-8 (pbk.)
    1. Mountains—Juvenile literature. [1. Mountains.] I. Camm, Martin, ill. II. Title. III. Series.
GB512.V72   1990
508.314'3—dc20   89-20299

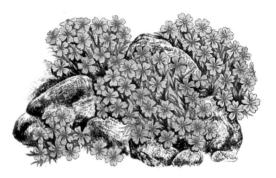

Map: Major mountain ranges of the world

Title page:
Sunset in the Himalayas

CONTENTS

The World's High Places

For many people, mountains are the world's best playgrounds. In winter, the thrills and spills of skiing attract thousands of people. In summer, tourists hike across the lower slopes, or just admire the spectacular scenery, and expeditions set off to the most challenging peaks.

The world's highest peak is Mount Everest, in the Himalayas. Until it was climbed in 1953, it was one of the Earth's last unconquered frontiers. Since the 1920s, at least a dozen expeditions had tried to reach the summit without success.

In many countries, mountains are regarded as holy places. In 1955, the Maharajah, or ruler, of Sikkim agreed to an expedition up Mount Kanchenjunga in the Himalayas — but only if the climbers stopped short of the summit, the sacred home of the mountain gods.

Some mountainous regions are so remote that life there has changed little over the ages. In Papua New Guinea, near Australia, some tribes still live much as they did in the Stone Age. Each tribe is so isolated that 750 languages are spoken in the one country.

Mountains may be solitary peaks or part of long ranges. They can affect the weather over huge regions.

→ The highest peaks in four continents:

Asia: Mount Everest
29,028 feet
North America: Mount McKinley
20,320 feet
Africa: Mount Kilimanjaro
19,565 feet
Europe: Mount Elbrus
18,481 feet

Everest
29,028 feet

McKinley
20,320 feet

Kilimanjaro
19,565 feet

4

↑ Walking in the Himalayas, the highest mountain range in the world.

Elbrus
18,481 feet

Lush coastland on one side of the mountain range may contrast with bleak desert on the other. Mountains can also be an obstacle to travel, as the early American settlers discovered when their first wagon trains reached the Rockies.

How Mountains are Formed

The Earth's surface, or *crust*, is made of hard rock. If the Earth was an apple, the crust would be no thicker than the apple's skin. The crust is broken up into pieces, like a gigantic jigsaw puzzle. Some of these pieces, or *plates*, are continents. Others are the ocean floors.

Beneath the Earth's surface there is a layer of *molten*, or liquid, rock. Currents in this hot, soft rock push and pull the plates floating on the surface. As a result, the continents and oceans are constantly moving, though they only shift a few inches every year.

When two plates collide, their edges buckle and are squeezed together, forming chains of mountains. Millions of years ago, India was separated from the rest of Asia by an ocean called the Tethys Sea. Gradually, the currents of hot, liquid rock beneath the Earth's surface pushed the Indian plate closer to the rest of Asia. The Tethys Sea narrowed and finally disappeared. Rocks from the ocean floor and those at the edges of the Indian and Asian plates slowly crumpled and built up into the Himalayan chain.

fold

6

→ The continents of the Earth, about 80-100 million years ago. Then, an ocean called the Tethys Sea separated Africa and India from Euro-Asia. As the African plate moved closer to Europe, the Tethys Sea shrank. Rocks were folded, or buckled, and rose to form the Alps, Pyrenees, and Atlas mountains. The Indian plate also collided with Euro-Asia, making the great Himalayan Range. The Tethys Sea became closed in.

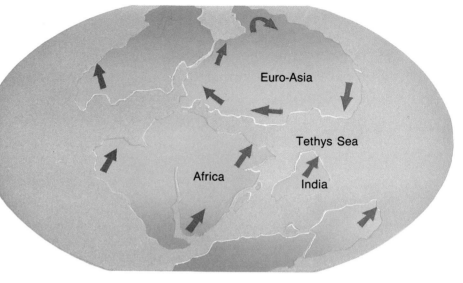

Euro-Asia

Tethys Sea

Africa

India

↓ When two plates collide, great thicknesses of rock are squashed together. As they are squeezed, they fold and bend to form mountain ranges, or they crack, forming *faults*. Where the pressure squeezes a mass of land upward, a block mountain (or *horst*) is formed. The rocks between faults may slip down to create a *rift valley*.

Not all mountains are created by plates colliding. In regions where the Earth's crust is torn, molten rock oozes through the cracks and builds up into volcanic mountains. The mountains around the Great Rift Valley, which divides the continent of Africa, were formed this way.

block mountain (horst)

rift valley

7

There are many types of volcanoes, and their activity continues to change the world's landscape. Most are under the oceans, where some mountain peaks are even taller than Mount Everest. Some islands, like Hawaii and Iceland, are the summits of massive underwater volcanoes jutting out above the ocean's surface.

The collision that created the Himalayas happened over 60 million years ago. It is not yet over, and the mountains are still rising. The world's other great ranges – the Andes, the Alps, and the Rockies – are of similar age. But there are much older mountains. The American Appalachians, the Scottish Highlands, and the Russian Urals were all formed over 250 million years ago. Today, these mountains have soft, rounded shapes, but once they were towering, jagged peaks.

As soon as mountains rise upward, they are attacked by wind, rain, frost, snow, and ice. These elements wear away the mountains in a process known as *erosion*. Rivers and glaciers speed up the action, carving deep valleys and sweeping away rocks. It seems incredible that mountains can simply vanish, but millions of years from now, the world's highest peaks will have been worn down to flat plains.

8

← People have found the remains of sea creatures and shells, like those shown here, in the rocks on top of mountains. These fossils were first formed on the bottom of the sea. They were carried upward as mountains were created by two plates colliding.

↑ Gentle hills and soaring peaks in the Andes, in Peru. The higher mountains are above the snowline. This is an imaginary line, but above it there is always snow on the ground both in winter and in summer. The great Andes Range stretches for 4,500 miles in South America.

9

Rocks and Minerals

The Earth is a great ball of rock, weighing about 6,600,000,000,000,000,000,000,000 (6.6 sextillion) tons! A grain of sand is a tiny rock. Even soil is mostly broken-down rock. Rocks are made of many different minerals. Neither plant nor animal, minerals are naturally created chemical substances.

We can understand how mountains are formed by studying the rocks they are made of. The beautiful marble we quarry was molded by heat and pressure. Rock that has changed its form like this is *metamorphic rock.* Deposits of sand, mud and shells of millions of tiny sea creatures on the ocean bottom harden into what we call *sedimentary rock. Igneous rock* is formed from rocks that have been heated so intensely that they have melted. This rock lies beneath all the other rocks of the Earth. It is the base of continents, the floor of oceans, and the core of mountains. Basalt is one common type of igneous rock.

↑ Two *igneous rocks.* Obsidian (1) is a glassy, black rock formed on the surface of the Earth from hardened volcanic lava. Granite (2) is a coarse-grained rock which forms in huge underground masses.

10

← Coal (3) comes from decayed plant remains. It was formed in ancient swamps. Limestone (4), sandstone (5), and conglomerates (6) are *sedimentary rocks*, formed from deposits of sand, mud, and sea shells. Conglomerates consist of rounded fragments of other rocks cemented in sand.

↑ A marble quarry at Carrara in Italy. Carrara is famous for its pure white marble, which was used by the sculptor Michelangelo.

→ Marble is a *metamorphic rock*. It is formed by the action of great heat and pressure on limestone.

11

The Himalayas

The Himalayas stretch across five countries in the heart of Asia: India, China, Tibet, Bhutan and Nepal. They include Mount Everest, the world's tallest mountain, and more than a hundred other peaks over 23,000 feet high. Before the 1960s, few people visited this remote and fascinating region. Today tourists go trekking in the mountains, and every year there are dozens of climbing expeditions.

↑ Yaks are expert climbers and live high on craggy Himalayan slopes. Local people depend on them for milk and transport.

Nepal is the home of the Sherpas, the famous mountaineers and guides who farm high in the Himalayas. After harvest, they trek over the steep passes carrying cereals and other goods to sell in Tibet, then return with heavy loads of salt and wool.

The Himalayas are not all snow-capped mountains. The foothills rising from the Indus and Ganges river valleys enjoy long hot summers and mild winters. Monkeys swing through the dense forests, and banana trees line the roadsides. As you climb, the climate becomes drier and colder. Red pandas and black and brown bears live in the higher pine forests, while yaks, goats, and wild sheep roam dry, rocky areas. Above the snowline, small, furry hares, marmots and voles are hunted by the mountain tiger, the rare and beautiful snow leopard, and the soaring golden eagle.

12

← The red panda **(far left)** lives in the mountain forests of the Himalayas. It feeds on roots, nuts, and bamboo shoots. The snow leopard **(left)** lives only on the snowline of the Himalayas. It is one of the most beautiful and endangered of the world's big cats.

↑ Sherpa villagers meeting under a pipal tree. These people of Nepal speak a Tibetan dialect. They are farmers, cattle breeders, and traders, and also spin and weave woolen cloth. Sherpas often act as guides and porters for Himalayan climbing expeditions.

13

↑ Walking in the Karakoram Range. These mountains form the border between Pakistan and China. It is easy to see why the name of the range means "black stones."

← Wild sheep climb around dry, rocky areas in the Himalayas.

The most famous inhabitant of the Himalayas is probably the "abominable snowman." He is described as a primitive ape-like man covered with blonde or reddish hair. The Sherpas call him the *yeti*, or "dweller among rocks." A few Western climbers have reported sightings, and photos have been taken of footprints so large that they can only be explained by the existence of an ape-like creature. However, no one has managed to photograph him and it is not known for certain whether the yeti really exists.

The world's second highest peak used to be called Mount Godwin Austen, but is now known as K2. It is part of the Karakoram Range, which is linked to the Himalayas. Hardly anything grows in this cold mountain desert, and almost no one lives there. It is one of the unfriendliest places in the world.

The Karakoram Pass is the highest point on what was once an important trade route between India and China. Karakoram means "black stones." Skeletons of dead pack animals litter the pass, and some of the world's most experienced mountaineers have died climbing the peaks that surround it.

↑ Are these the footprints of the famous *yeti* or "abominable snowman?" No one knows for certain if the creature really exists.

← The Himalayan black bear lives in the higher pine forests.

15

At the dry western end of the Himalayas, the Hindu Kush mountains stretch into Afghanistan and Pakistan. The Hindu Kush is a parched, brown, lifeless wilderness. Few trees grow there except in sheltered valleys around villages. For half the year, even these valleys are snowbound, and there is little for people to do except huddle around their fires. Wood is so scarce that they have to burn animal dung to keep warm.

The Himalayas have been damaged by poor farming methods. Many trees have been felled to make room for new fields to grow crops, or just to provide fuel. But without trees, the good soil washes away. Trees soak up water from the ground. Without them, water sweeps down the slopes into the valleys, swelling rivers and flooding central plains well beyond the mountains.

Bangladesh is a poor, crowded, flat country between the Himalayas and the Indian Ocean. When the monsoon winds bring heavy rains, there are regular floods. New trees are being planted on the Himalayas, but it will be a long time before the damage is repaired.

↑ Rain falls when moist air becomes cooler as it rises over mountains (top). When too many trees are cut down, rains wash away the exposed soil. Rain and soil sweep down into valleys and plains (middle). The mountainside is left bare, with few plants and no animals (bottom).

→ Sherpa women in the Kathmandu Valley, Nepal, carrying firewood. In other areas of the Himalayas, so many trees have been cut down that wood is hard to find.

The Andes

The Andes are the backbone of South America, running along the west coast right down to Cape Horn. Although they are regarded as the Earth's longest mountain chain, the Andes are actually several ranges linked by *plateaus*, or highland plains.

The landscape has some dramatic features, including several of the world's highest volcanoes and Lake Titicaca,

the world's highest navigable lake. One way to enjoy the spectacular scenery is to travel on Peru's Central Railroad, which zigzags up to almost 16,500 feet.

Almost a third of all South Americans live in the Andes — some in cities, others in villages that have hardly changed in centuries. The capitals of four countries are high up in the Andes: La Paz (in Bolivia), Quito (Ecuador), Bogotá (Colombia) and Caracas (Venezuela).

↑ The llama is a sure-footed, hardy animal. It is kept by farmers in the Andes for meat and wool.

↑ Miners arriving for work at a tin mine in Bolivia in the Andes. Tin mining is the country's most important industry.

← Lake Titicaca lies on a high plateau between Peru and Bolivia. The local people make boats from reeds that grow around the shores of the lake. The canoe-shaped boats have been made in the same way for centuries.

19

Up in the mountains the air is thinner than in low-lying areas and contains less oxygen. As a result, visitors often feel dizzy. But people who live high up do not suffer from mountain sickness. They have a richer supply of red blood cells, so they can take in more oxygen from the thin mountain air. Before tackling a major climb, mountaineers train at a high altitude to allow their bodies to adjust. However, oxygen masks are often needed for climbing high peaks.

Life is so hard in mountainous regions that most civilizations have developed in lowland areas. One remarkable exception was the empire of the Incas, which once flourished in the Andes. When Francisco Pizarro and his Spanish soldiers, called *conquistadores*, arrived there in 1532 it was larger than any European kingdom. The emperor, known simply as the Inca, ruled over possibly 16 million people, yet he was conquered by Pizarro's 180 soldiers.

↑ The condor is a huge vulture found high in the Andes. It has a wingspan of 10 feet, and swoops down on lambs and young deer.

One of the few remains of this vanished empire is Machu Picchu in Peru, where Inca farmers cut thousands of terraces into the steep hillsides so they could grow crops. The Inca capital, Cuzco, also in Peru, was known as the "city of gold," because gold was so plentiful in the surrounding hills.

← Machu Picchu, Peru. These Inca ruins were discovered in 1911. As well as farming terraces, they include a royal palace and a sun temple made of stone blocks.

The Rockies

The Rocky Mountains stretch along the western part of the North American continent from New Mexico to northern Alaska. Desert regions lie to the west of the range, and great plains to the east. The highest part of the range is in Colorado, which today boasts some of the finest ski resorts in the United States. Mount Elbert, in central Colorado, is the tallest peak.

↑ Indian cliff dwellings in Arizona. Hopi Indians built stone towns on these rocky plateaus.

For more than 400 years, from the end of the 15th century, explorers searched for the Northwest Passage — a sea or river route from the Atlantic to the Pacific, so trading ships could reach China more quickly. They were unaware that the northern end of the Rockies stood between them and their dream.

Most of the exploration of the Rockies was done in the 19th century by fur traders and trappers called "the mountain men." By the 1850s, very few animals were left and the fur trade was dying. But the mountain men found a new way of earning a living. They knew the mountains so well that they were able to help mapmakers charting the region, and guide wagon trains through the Rockies as settlers moved west.

→ Skiing in the Rockies, on fresh powder snow.

← The mountain lion, also called the puma or cougar, is a muscular animal with a powerful leap. It feeds on goats, deer, and mountain sheep. It took to the mountains to survive attacks by early human settlers.

↑ A farm in the Rockies near Denver, Colorado.

The first mountain trails were made by animals such as deer and buffalo. Indians learned to track them, and the mountain men followed the Indian trails. Missionaries and thousands of farmers who had been experiencing hard times in the Midwest were guided to the lush pastures of the West by the mountain men. Some of the routes pioneered by the new settlers were then followed by the railroad builders.

Today, large areas of the Rockies are preserved as national parks, and the wildlife there is protected. The Rocky Mountain goat clambers over craggy peaks, shielded from the winter cold by its thick fur. Marmots and grizzly bears survive the winters by *hibernating*, or going into a long, deep sleep. Eagles glide around the peaks, using their sharp eyesight to spot prey far below, while vultures rely on their keen sense of smell. Other fierce hunters of the Rockies are the coyote and the mountain lion, which preys on deer and elk.

→ The Rocky Mountain goat has sharp horns and a silky coat. It is quite at home on steep rocky ledges.

← The grizzly is a large brown bear of the mountains. It eats meat, fruit, berries, and honey, and can be over 8 feet tall.

25

The Alps

The Alps are the youngest of the world's great mountain ranges. They form a barrier between the Mediterranean and northern Europe, stretching across France, Italy, Switzerland, Germany, Austria, Yugoslavia, Albania, and tiny Liechtenstein.

During the last Ice Age, about 10,000 years ago, frozen rivers, or *glaciers*, carved deep valleys through the mountains. Debris dragged along by the glaciers piled up into *moraines*, or mounds, at the head of the valleys. As the ice melted, finger-shaped lakes, such as Lake Como and Lake Maggiore in Italy, formed behind the moraines, which acted as natural dams.

The Alps include hundreds of peaks higher than 10,000 feet, some 1,200 glaciers, and about 50 passes. The tallest peak in the Alps is Mont Blanc. Beneath it, one of Europe's longest road tunnels links France with Italy. The Rhine and many other European rivers begin with melting snow from the Alps.

↑ Spruce **(left)**, and fir **(right)**. These hardy, needle-leaved trees are typical of Alpine slopes.

For centuries, Alpine farms have produced milk, cream, and cheeses. In summer, the cows graze peacefully on the fresh grass of the highland meadows. But in winter it is too cold for them to stay out in the open, so they are brought down to the valleys. There they live in barns and feed on hay.

Glacier buttercup

26

← Alpine plants have specially adapted to withstand the cold and exposed conditions found on steep mountainsides. They are usually compact and springy, like the glacier buttercup shown here.

↑ Alpine huts used for storing hay, in Zermatt Valley, Switzerland. The hay is used for feeding cows in winter.

→ The ibex is a rare type of wild goat that lives in the Alps. It stays above the timberline all the year round.

27

The lower slopes of the Alps are covered with crops, vineyards, and orchards. Then come forests of pine, spruce, and fir trees. Above these there are grassy meadows, which are dotted in spring and summer with small tufts of colorful Alpine flowers. Despite their fragile looks, these short-stemmed plants are very hardy. Some contain a fluid that acts like antifreeze, which saves them from freezing. One plant, the Alpine snowbell, even produces enough heat to melt snow. Above the meadows loom craggy rocks and snow-clad peaks that only ibex and chamois can climb.

↑ Avalanches can happen suddenly. Climbers and skiers should always treat mountains with caution.

Mountains may be picturesque, but they must be treated with caution. A clear, sunny day can become cloudy, snowy, or freezing within minutes. Snow brings with it the danger of avalanches. These can vary from a cascade of powdery snow to a massive slide of hard snow and ice that hurtles down the mountainside at over 60 miles per hour. Avalanches are often caused by a heavy fall of snow, but they can be triggered by skiing, or gunfire, or even by someone shouting.

Despite these dangers, sports such as mountaineering and skiing are enjoyed wherever there are peaks to climb or slopes covered with snow.

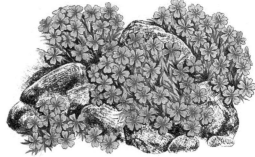

Moss campion

28

← The moss campion's round, small shape protects it from the wind. Its mass of shapely leaves retain heat at night. Edelweiss is one of the most well-known and beautiful Alpine plants. About 6 inches high, it belongs to the daisy family.

Edelweiss

↑ Climbing a rock face near Mont Blanc, the highest mountain in the Alps. In the mountains, a clear day like this can turn to bad weather within minutes.

Fact File

What is a Mountain?
To geographers and scientists, a mountain is a hill that rises 1,000 feet or more above the surrounding land.

Highest Mountain Range
The Himalayan range is 2,400 miles long and includes more than 100 peaks over 23,000 feet high.

The five highest peaks are:

Everest 29,028 feet
K2 (Godwin Austen)
   28,250 feet
Kanchenjunga 28,146 feet
Lhotse 27,890 feet
Makalu 27,790 feet

Highest Peaks in Each Continent
Africa: Kilimanjaro (Tanzania)
   19,565 feet
Antarctica: Vinson Massif
   (Sentinel Range)
   16,285 feet
Asia: Everest (Nepal/China)
   29,028 feet
Australasia: Kosciusko
   (Australia) 7,305 feet
Europe: Elbrus (U.S.S.R.)
   18,481 feet
North America: McKinley
   (Alaska) 20,320 feet
South America: Aconcagua
   (Argentina/Chile)
   22,835 feet

↑ *Meeting of two large glaciers on Mont Blanc, in the Alps*

↓ *Mount Everest* (center)

30

Longest Mountain Ranges
Andes (South America)
 4,500 miles
Rocky Mountains (North
 America) 3,750 miles
Himalayas (Asia) 2,400 miles

Highest Capital Cities
The highest capital city in the world is Lhasa, Tibet. It is 12,000 feet above sea level. The second highest is La Paz, Bolivia, at 11,900 feet.

Longest Mountain Tunnels
The longest railway tunnel bored through a mountain is the Simplon Tunnel linking Switzerland and Italy. Cut through the Alps, it is 12 miles long.

The longest mountain road tunnel is the St. Gotthard Road Tunnel in Switzerland. It is 10 miles long.

Mountain Weather
As you go up a mountain, the temperature falls about 4°F for every 1,000 feet you climb.

The world's highest wind speed (excluding hurricanes and tornadoes) was recorded on the upper slopes of Mount Washington, New Hampshire. On April 12, 1934 the wind there reached 230 miles per hour.

The deepest snow ever reported was also on a mountain: 28 feet on Lassen Peak, California, in 1983.

Mountain Animals
Yaks (long-haired oxen) are the only kind of cattle fully adapted to living at high altitudes. In the mountains of China and Tibet, they sometimes climb to 20,000 feet in search of food.

In the Himalayas, the Apollo butterfly has been spotted flying as high as 18,000 feet.

Mountaineering
Today the 30 highest peaks in the world have been climbed, but mountaineering has only been popular as a sport for about 200 years.

In 1787, Horace Benedict de Saussure climbed Mont Blanc, the highest peak in the Alps. This encouraged other mountaineers, and by 1865 most of the other Alpine peaks had been climbed.

The best-known of all mountaineering triumphs took place on May 29, 1953. That morning, Sherpa Tenzing Norgay and New Zealander Edmund Hillary became the first climbers to reach the summit of Everest. At the summit, Hillary buried a small crucifix in the snow, and Tenzing left some chocolate as a gift to the mountain gods.

↓ *Climbing in the Rockies*

Index

Picture Credits
John Beatty: pages 12-13, 15, 24-25, 31
Hutchison Library: Jeremy Horner 16-17;
Brian Moser 18-19; Robert Francis 20-21;
A.F. Howland 22
Mountain Camera: John Cleare 4-5, 8-9,
14-15, 26-27, 28, 28-29,
30 (top & bottom); Lanny Johnson 22-23
Survival Anglia: Dieter & Mary Plage 1
A.C. Waltham: 10-11